Mountain Wolf Woman

Other Badger Biographies

Belle and Bob La Follette: Partners in Politics
Caroline Quarlls and the Underground Railroad
Casper Jaggi: Master Swiss Cheese Maker
Curly Lambeau: Building the Green Bay Packers
Dr. Kate: Angel on Snowshoes
Frank Lloyd Wright and His New American Architecture
Gaylord Nelson: Champion for Our Earth
Harley and the Davidsons: Motorcycle Legends
Mai Ya's Long Journey
Ole Evinrude and His Outboard Motor
A Recipe for Success: Lizzie Kander and Her Cookbook
Richard Bong: World War II Flying Ace
Tents, Tigers, and the Ringling Brothers

Mountain Wolf Woman
A Ho-Chunk Girlhood

Diane Young Holliday

Wisconsin Historical Society Press

Published by the Wisconsin Historical Society Press
Publishers since 1855

© 2007 by State Historical Society of Wisconsin

All rights reserved. No part of this book may be reproduced in any manner or in any medium without written permission from the publisher, except by reviewers, who may quote brief passages in critical articles and reviews. To request permission to reprint passages or quote from this copyrighted work, write to Permissions, Wisconsin Historical Society Press, 816 State Street, Madison, WI 53706.

wisconsin**history**.org

Photographs identified with PH, WHi, or WHS are from the Society's collections; address inquiries about such photos to the Visual Materials Archivist at the above address.

Printed in the United States of America
Designed by Jill Bremigan

13 12 11 10 09   2 3 4 5 6

Library of Congress Cataloging-in-Publication Data

Holliday, Diane Young, 1951–
  Mountain Wolf Woman : a Ho-Chunk girlhood / Diane Young Holliday.
    p. cm. — (Badger biographies)
  Includes bibliographical references and index.
  ISBN 978-0-87020-381-7 (pbk. : alk. paper) 1. Mountain Wolf Woman, 1884–1960—Juvenile literature. 2. Ho Chunk women—Biography—Juvenile literature. 3. Ho Chunk Indians—Biography—Juvenile literature. 4. Ho Chunk Indians—Social life and customs—Juvenile literature. 5. Wisconsin—Social life and customs—Juvenile literature. I. Title.
  E99.W7H65 2007
  977.5004'975260092—dc22
   [B]
                    2007002539

Front cover photo: WHi Image ID 9385
Back cover photo: WHS Museum Object ID: 1998.241.45, A
The image of Jean Nicolet on page 3 is part of a mural in the Wisconsin Historical Society in Madison, Wisconsin.

∞ The paper used in this publication meets the minimum requirements of the American National Standard for Information Sciences—Permanence of Paper for Printed Library Materials, ANSI Z39.48-1992.

To my daughter Xi He Ping,
who has taught me so
much in her own journey
through childhood

Contents

1 Meet Mountain Wolf Woman and Her People 1
2 The Gift of a Name 16
3 Following the Seasons: Spring and Summer 24
4 Following the Seasons: Fall and Winter 38
5 Many Ways of Growing Up 51
      Afterword 65
      Appendix: Mountain Wolf Woman's Time Line 67
      Glossary 68
      Reading Group Guide and Activities 71
      To Learn More about the Ho-Chunk 73
      Acknowledgments 74
      Index 75

FROM MOUNTAIN WOLF WOMAN: SISTER OF CRASHING THUNDER: THE AUTOBIOGRAPHY OF A WINNEBAGO INDIAN, EDITED BY NANCY OESTREICH LURIE

1
Meet Mountain Wolf Woman and Her People

When Mountain Wolf Woman was born in April of 1884, Wisconsin had been a state for only 36 years. Although Wisconsin was a young state, Mountain Wolf Woman's people, the Ho-Chunk Nation, had lived in Wisconsin for hundreds, probably even thousands, of years. They live here still.

Mountain Wolf Woman grew up at a time when the Ho-Chunk way of living remained much like that of her **ancestors**. But other parts of her life were very different. This is the way it is for all families. Think of the many ways your life is both different from and the same as that of your grandparents and great-grandparents and great-great-grandparents.

ancestor: a family member from long ago

Nancy Oestreich Lurie

Nancy Lurie

To learn about Mountain Wolf Woman's life in her own words, read *Mountain Wolf Woman: Sister of Crashing Thunder; The Autobiography of a Winnebago Indian* edited by Nancy Oestreich Lurie. Nancy Lurie is an **anthropologist** (an thro **pah** lo jist). She has studied the history and **culture** of the Ho-Chunk people.

When Nancy Lurie was a college student, she was adopted by one of Mountain Wolf Woman's relatives and became the niece of Mountain Wolf Woman. This kind of adoption among Indian people is a special form of friendship. As the friend becomes one of the family, the friend assumes the duties and **privileges** of all family members. These duties and privileges are determined by how one person is related to another. For example, aunts are expected to treat nieces and nephews with special **generosity**. So, when Nancy Lurie asked for Mountain Wolf Woman's life story, she happily told it in her own language, and Lurie recorded it.

Lurie then turned to a Ho-Chunk friend, Frances Thundercloud, who speaks Ho-Chunk and English equally well. Frances Thundercloud **translated** Mountain Wolf Woman's Ho-Chunk words into English. When you see quotes in this book, they are Mountain Wolf Woman's words translated into English.

---

anthropologist: a scientist who studies human history by looking at the languages people speak; the environment in which they live; and the way they work, dress, eat, create art, and construct buildings   **culture:** the way of life, ideas, and traditions of a group of people   **privilege:** a special right   **generosity:** helping others by sharing things such as time or money   **translated:** put in a different language

The first European to arrive in the western Great Lakes region was Jean Nicolet (jhan nik oh **lay**) in 1634. He was sent by the French government in Canada. But the French did not return to what is now Wisconsin for another 30 years because they were fighting the Iroquois (**ear** eh kwoy), Indian people who lived in eastern North America. When the French did travel back to Wisconsin in the 1660s, they came to set up missions and trading posts.

For generations before the Europeans' arrival, Ho-Chunk families planted gardens of corn, beans, and squash, and they gathered many wild plants for food. They also caught fish and hunted animals with bows and arrows. They made their own clothes from tanned animal skins and built their own houses with bark or cattail mats.

There were no cameras when Jean Nicolet visited Wisconsin in the 1600s; this is what an artist nearly 300 years later imagined he looked like.

Each year, as the seasons came and went, groups of Ho-Chunk people moved to rivers, to woods, and to fields to get the foods and materials that they needed to live.

Ho-Chunk garden in winter

But when the French arrived in North America, Ho-Chunk life began to change.

The Indians traded furs from animals they trapped for European goods such as kettles, knives, guns, cloth, and beads. Before the fur trade, the Ho-Chunk had been living in a large settlement in the Green Bay area. Once the French arrived, the Ho-Chunk began forming smaller villages. They spread across southwestern Wisconsin and northwestern Illinois in order to trap beaver and other animals along the many area rivers, including the Fox, Wisconsin, Rock, and Black.

The Ho-Chunk used European beads to decorate bags like this one from more recent times.

When the British took control of North America from the French in 1763, they continued trading with the Indians. And when the Americans took control from the British after the Revolutionary War, they also continued trading with the Indians. But then the American settlers wanted more than just trade. They wanted land. But different groups of Native people already lived all over the Americas. Many, of course, lived in what became the state of Wisconsin. How did the United States government deal with that problem?

More than 50 years before Mountain Wolf Woman was born, the United States government decided to move as many Indians as possible across the Mississippi River. Most tribes had little choice but to sign **treaties** to sell their land and move to other land set aside for them.

Members of the Ho-Chunk Nation were forced to give up their homeland in Wisconsin and Illinois in exchange for a **reservation** in Iowa. Then, in a series of treaties, the Ho-Chunk people were moved to Minnesota, South Dakota, and, finally, Nebraska. Today, about half of the Ho-Chunk people still live in Nebraska.

treaty: an official, written agreement between nations   **reservation:** federal land reserved or set aside for Indian nations to live on

Meet Mountain Wolf Woman and Her People

Imagine how you would feel if the government told your family that you had to move away from everything you knew and live in a land you had never seen!

How many times were the Ho-Chunk forced to move?

Some Ho-Chunk families refused to leave. They preferred to hide out in their beloved Wisconsin. Some who left Wisconsin returned later, including Mountain Wolf Woman's family.

Where Does the Name Ho-Chunk Come From?

The name Ho-Chunk can mean either "big fish" or "big voice." This is big in the sense of important or original. You may have heard of the name Winnebago. This is what some people used to call the Ho-Chunk. Winnebago came from a Mesquakie (mes **kwaw** kee) Indian word meaning "people of the stinking water." The Ho-Chunk used to live near marshy areas around Green Bay and the Fox River. These waters sometimes filled with very smelly dead fish and **algae** (al jee) in the spring. Ho-Chunk is a name that comes from the Ho-Chunk language; in other words, this is a name they call themselves.

algae: small plants with roots or stems that live in water or on damp surfaces

In 1874, 10 years before Mountain Wolf Woman was born, U.S. government officials put her family, along with other Ho-Chunk people, on a train. The train took them to Nebraska to live on the tribe's reservation there. Mountain Wolf Woman's mother, named Bends the Bough, later told her that some Ho-Chunk did not want to leave Wisconsin. But Bends the Bough said she was happy because she would see some of her relatives who had been moved earlier.

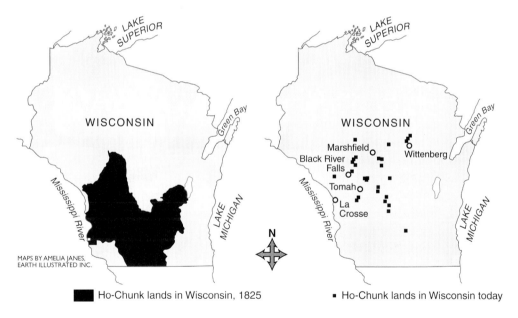

■ Ho-Chunk lands in Wisconsin, 1825   ■ Ho-Chunk lands in Wisconsin today

Compare the amount of land under Ho-Chunk control in 1825 and today. How do you think the U.S. government was successful in getting the land it wanted?

Meet Mountain Wolf Woman and Her People

It was winter when Bends the Bough and her family arrived in Nebraska. They quickly built **wigwams** to keep warm. Wigwams were a handy type of house that could be built quickly in different sizes. Indian people in eastern North America had been building wigwams for thousands of years.

To build their wigwams, Mountain Wolf Woman's family members cut down small saplings and stuck them into the ground to make round or oval shapes. Then they pulled the saplings down toward the middle and tied them together to

Like houses today, wigwams came in all sizes.

wigwam: a home made of cattail mats or tree bark attached to a framework of small branches

8

form arches. They tied other saplings around the arches. After building these frames, they covered the outside with mats made from cattail plants or large pieces of elm or birch bark. Inside the wigwam, they covered the floor with mats made from bulrushes. These floor mats were harder to make. They also used these mats for decoration. A fireplace in the wigwam provided heat and light. A well-built wigwam was very comfortable.

But when the next spring arrived, many people were dying on the reservation in Nebraska. It was cold, and there were diseases and hunger. Somebody died almost every day! There were many burials and many tears. Bends the Bough was frightened for her family. She asked, "Why do we stay here? I am afraid because the people are all dying. Why do we not go back home?" So she and other family members decided to return to their homeland in Wisconsin. They moved to the Missouri River. There, they cut down big willow trees and made **dugout canoes** to prepare for their journey home.

dugout canoe: a boat made by hollowing out a large log

Dugout Canoes

Dugout canoes were made from a single log. Before the Indians got metal tools through the fur trade, they used fire to hollow out a large log. They burned the wood and then scraped away the charred wood with tools made from stone and shell. Later, after Indians began trade with Europeans, they used metal tools.

The dugout canoe has a long history in Wisconsin waters. **Archaeologists** (ar key ol o jists) from the Wisconsin Historical Society have preserved the remains of 2 dugout canoes—one is about 150 years old and the other is 1,800 years old!

Dugout canoe

Drawing of the 150-year-old dugout canoe preserved by archaeologists

archaeologist: a scientist who learns about the past by studying artifacts or objects left behind at places where people once lived, worked, and played

To return home to Wisconsin, Mountain Wolf Woman's family first paddled down the Missouri River to the "River's Mouth Place," where St. Louis, Missouri, is today. From River's Mouth Place, they paddled up the Mississippi River. Finally, the family made it to Prairie du Chien and then to La Crosse. From La Crosse, they moved to Black River Falls.

How long do you think this dugout canoe trip took Mountain Wolf Woman's family?

Have you ever floated *down* a river on an inner tube? You float *with* the current. Can you imagine paddling *up* the Mississippi River *against* the current of North America's largest river? Think of how strong you'd have to be! Mountain Wolf Woman's family must have really wanted to get home to Wisconsin.

The River's Mouth Place

The Ho-Chunk called St. Louis "River's Mouth Place" because it is there that the waters of the Missouri River empty into the Mississippi River, and this is called the Missouri's "mouth." But do you know why this place is called St. Louis today? This part of America was once owned by France. In 1764, a French fur trader established a trading post at this spot. He named it after his French king, Louis XV, and that is the name that most people have used since then.

After the 1874 attempt to remove all the Ho-Chunk from Wisconsin, the U.S. government gave up. The very next year, the government allowed the Ho-Chunk people who had returned to Wisconsin to live in their traditional homeland. Those who chose to return to Wisconsin could claim a **homestead**. Earlier, in 1862, the U.S. Congress had passed a law that allowed some people to get a homestead of 160 acres of land. In the 1870s and 1880s, Congress changed the law to include Indians. The new law was supposed to encourage them to live like non-Indian farmers.

But private ownership of land had not been part of Ho-Chunk life in the past. The Ho-Chunk people were used to planting large gardens on tribal lands each spring, and then they moved to different areas of their territory to get other types of foods throughout the year. Mountain Wolf Woman's father was definitely not interested in owning any land because he was a member of a sky **clan**—the Thunder Clan. Mountain Wolf Woman remembered him saying, "I do not belong to the earth and I have no concern with land."

homestead: land given by the U.S. government to settlers if they built a home and began farming within 5 years
clan: a group of people with a common sacred ancestor, such as an animal or spirit

Bends the Bough was also a member of a sky clan, the Eagle Clan. But she had her own ideas. She decided that in those changing times the family needed a place to call its own. She took a 40-acre homestead near Black River Falls. Mountain Wolf Woman's father built a log cabin on the homestead. Mountain Wolf Woman's family lived there during parts of the year, but often the family went away to get food or earn money.

Black River Falls when Mountain Wolf Woman was a child

Clans

Like many other Indian nations, Ho-Chunk society is organized by clans. The clans in Ho-Chunk society, as in some other Indian cultures, are divided into at least 2 groups: those who are on earth and those who are above—the earth and sky.

The largest Ho-Chunk sky clan is the Thunder Clan. The Eagle, Hawk, and Pigeon are also sky clans. The earth division includes the Bear Clan as well as the Water Spirit, Fish, Buffalo, Deer, Elk, Snake, and Wolf clans. Clans are named for the animal spirit ancestor. Each clan has its own **origin** story. The Ho-Chunk people believe that long ago, **spiritual** (**spir** i chooel) beings, who could take animal or human form, founded the clans.

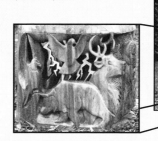

The Ho-Chunk Family *Tree by Ho-Chunk artist Harry Whitehorse shows the Ho-Chunk earth and sky clans. This sculpture is at Thoreau Elementary School in Madison, Wisconsin.*

Traditionally, different clans are responsible for different tasks. In the past, the Bear Clan kept order in the villages and made decisions about land. Peace chiefs came from the Thunder Clan. Today, clans are still important. The clans have responsibilities at feasts and **ceremonies** (**ser** uh mo neez).

---

origin: where something comes from   **spiritual:** something that has to do with the soul and the spirit
ceremony: formal words, actions, or songs that mark an important special occasion, such as a wedding or a funeral

2

The Gift of a Name

Mountain Wolf Woman's early childhood years were not recorded in photographs or videos as are those of many children today. But much was stored in her memories and in the memories of her family. Back in the 1880s, most people were born at home rather than in hospitals. From her family, she knew that she was born at her grandfather's house at a place called East Fork River. It was early spring when she took her first breath, and her family was making maple sugar.

For many Indian people in Wisconsin, making maple sugar was part of their yearly round of activities. It was something they did every spring. Early in the season, when there was still snow, people set up camps out in the woods in groves of maple trees. They made cuts in the trees with axes and then put a piece of wood into the cut to guide the oozing sap into a bucket.

People spent many hours and days collecting buckets of sap. Then they poured the sap into large kettles. They boiled the sap in these large kettles for many, many hours until it began to **granulate**. Sugaring took a lot of hard work, but people looked forward to working with family and friends. Sugaring was also a time of celebration because everyone knew the cold days and nights of winter were almost over.

The buckets on these trees are collecting sap that will soon become maple sugar.

Sugaring was an important seasonal activity for many Wisconsin Indians.

Mountain Wolf Woman's first memory was of a spring day sometime after her first birthday. She was with her mother, Bends the Bough, and her older sister White Thunder. Mother and daughters had come to a creek that they needed to cross,

granulate: form crystals

and there was no bridge. Her mother had been carrying Mountain Wolf Woman on her back in a **cradleboard**. When babies are in cradleboards, they face backward and can't see where they are going. Mountain Wolf Woman started squirming. "I was restless," she remembered. Bends the Bough took her off the board and carried her in a shawl on her back. From the shawl, Mountain Wolf Woman looked over her mother's shoulder and saw what was happening. "I saw the water swirling swiftly." She remembered seeing White Thunder carry the empty cradleboard across the creek while she held her skirt up to keep it from getting wet.

When she was older, Mountain Wolf Woman told her mother about this memory and asked her if it had really happened. Bends the Bough was amazed that she had such an early memory—it was considered a sign of great intelligence! When Mountain Wolf Woman shared this story with her niece, Nancy Lurie, she did not want to sound as though she was bragging. Mountain Wolf Woman added that her mother suggested that she probably remembered this early moment because she was so frightened by the swift

cradleboard: a baby carrier used by American Indians

running water. Think back. What is your first memory? Was it something scary or some other strong feeling?

Cradleboards

All Ho-Chunk women kept their babies on cradleboards in the old days. The baby would be securely tied to a board with a footrest at one end and a hoop at the other end. The hoop was over the baby's head. It protected the child if the board should fall. The cradleboard was an easy way to carry babies. The boards could also be stood upright on the ground so the babies could watch what their families were doing. Mothers often hung beads or other bright objects on the hoop to entertain the baby. The cradleboard also made it easier for mothers to do their tasks. While the babies were kept snug and warm on the cradleboards, their mothers' hands were free to work.

Babies in cradleboards

Parents still use baby carriers to make life easier.

The Gift of a Name

Mountain Wolf Woman had several older sisters and brothers. It was the Ho-Chunk custom to have 2 names. One name was based on whether you were a girl or a boy and on the order of your birth in your family. Each person also had a **ceremonial** (ser uh **mo** nee uhl) name that usually came from the clan. If a family had more than 4 girls or boys, they began to use names that were forms of the first 4 names. In Ho-Chunk families, if a fifth daughter was born, like Mountain Wolf Woman, that girl's name was a form of the third girl's name. The chart shows the different names of the children in Mountain Wolf Woman's family.

Birth Order	Ho-Chunk Name	Ceremonial Name in Mountain Wolf Woman's Family
First Daughter	Hínuga (hee noo gah)	White Thunder
First Son	Kúnuga (koo noo gah)	Crashing Thunder
Second Daughter	Wihaŋga (wee hah hag)	Bald Eagle
Second Son	Hénaga (hay nah hag)	Strikes Standing
Third Daughter	Hakśigaga (hahk see gah)	No ceremonial name—this sister died very young.
Third Son	Hágaga (hah gah gah)	Big Winnebago
Fourth Daughter	Hinákega (hee nah kay gah)	Distant Flashes Standing
Fifth Daughter	Hakśigax̣unuga (hahk see gah koo noo)	Mountain Wolf Woman

ceremonial: formal or traditional

Mountain Wolf Woman got her ceremonial name when she was a little girl and was very, very sick. Bends the Bough was worried and did not know what to do. Finally, she asked an old woman named Wolf Woman to cure her daughter. Bends the Bough had great respect for the powers of old people. She told Wolf Woman, "I want my little girl to live. I give her to you. Whatever way you can make her live, she will be yours."

Among the Ho-Chunk people, highly valued possessions are to be given away, not kept for oneself. Of course, little Hakśigaxunuga was not a possession but the daughter of Bends the Bough. Giving her daughter to Wolf Woman to cure was both a way to help her baby and a way to honor Wolf Woman with a gift.

Wolf Woman cried at the thought of such a precious gift. Wolf Woman said, "My life, let her use it. My grandchild, let her use my existence." Then she gave the little child a holy name and predicted that she would live to be an old person. The name Wolf Woman gave the child was a Wolf Clan name—Xehaćiwiŋga (khay hah chee wee gah). And Xehaćiwiŋga got well! She lived to be an old person, just like Wolf Woman had said she would. Mountain Wolf Woman later said that the name Xehaćiwiŋga had a special meaning: "to make a home in a bluff or a mountain, as the wolf does, but in English I just say my name is Mountain Wolf Woman."

Although many children in Wisconsin went to school in the late 1800s, most Ho-Chunk children learned what they needed to know from their families. Very early, Mountain Wolf Woman learned how to behave politely and properly with family members as well as strangers. She also learned the importance of the many spirits in the Ho-Chunk world. She learned about her duty to **fast** in order to get blessings from the spirits. She learned to always listen to her parents and never to be lazy. Mountain Wolf Woman understood that someday when she became a mother herself, she should never hit or scold her children. The Ho-Chunk women taught their daughters that hitting or scolding showed poor parenting.

fast: go without food

Mountain Wolf Woman also spent many hours watching her mother and other women doing their work. She learned the things she would need to know to survive—how to garden, gather wild plants, and cook and preserve many kinds of food. She also learned how to build wigwams, prepare deer hides, make mats, weave baskets, and sew clothes.

These moccasins were made by Mountain Wolf Woman.

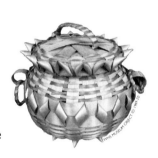

Ho-Chunk basket

Mountain Wolf Woman would have used thin strips of wood, like this piece, to weave baskets.

Ho-Chunk Spirits

The Ho-Chunk religion has many spirits, including Earthmaker, Thunder, Disease-Giver, Night Spirits, Sun, Moon, Day, Water Spirits, North Wind, South Wind, and Morning Star. The Ho-Chunk ask these spirits for blessings for good lives, health, and sometimes for "power"—the knowledge to heal and succeed.

3

Following the Seasons: Spring and Summer

When Mountain Wolf Woman was a girl, her parents did not have 8-hour-a-day jobs where they went to the same place and did the same thing every day. Her parents did not get paychecks and then go to stores to buy everything they needed. Ho-Chunk life followed the seasons. Where families went and what they did each day depended upon the time of year. They understood that different plants and animals were available in different places at different times. To survive, Mountain Wolf Woman's family had to have great knowledge about all plants and animals. It took planning and skill to live by hunting and gathering. And it was a good life. Her parents were their own bosses.

Ho-Chunk Month Names

The importance of the plants and animals and their seasons can be seen in the Ho-Chunk names for the months of the year.

> January—first bear month
> February—last bear month
> March—raccoon-breeding month
> April—fish becoming visible month
> May—drying of the earth month
> June—digging month
> July—**cultivating** month
> August—**tasseling** month
> September—elk-whistling month
> October—when the deer paw the earth month
> November—deer-breeding month
> December—when the deer shed their horns month

Why do we call the first month "January" or the last one "December"? How did we come by these names? Can you think of better ones?

cultivating: growing crops   **tasseling:** when the tassel, the part of a corn stalk with pollen on it, appears

In Mountain Wolf Woman's time, if you didn't want to go hungry, it was important to know the seasons of plants and the habits of animals. In the early spring, her family members trapped animals and sometimes made maple sugar when the sap ran. When the fields warmed, they planted large gardens of corn, beans, and squash. They picked berries and collected **tubers** when these plants were ready. They hunted deer, and sometimes bear, in the fall and early winter. And they stored food from their harvests and hunts to eat as they waited for the cold winter days to end.

The seasonal activities that Mountain Wolf Woman's family followed were much like what Ho-Chunk people had been doing for many generations. But in Wisconsin and across the United States, life was changing in the late 1800s. Non-Indian people were buying more and more land. Then they built fences to define and protect their property. Towns and cities were growing rapidly. It got harder and harder for Ho-Chunk people to live on just what they could grow or collect or hunt. In this changing world, Mountain Wolf Woman and her family also needed to earn money to buy things that they could no longer get from the land or make for themselves.

tuber: a root or bulb

Although Mountain Wolf Woman's family had its homestead near Black River Falls, the family members did not stay there all year. They spent several of the coldest winter months at home. Then they would start their trips to collect different foods. In March, they usually traveled to the Mississippi River near La Crosse. There, her father and uncles trapped lots of muskrats. These furry animals, sometimes called "marsh rabbits," were plentiful along the Mississippi and its **sloughs** (slooz). The Ho-Chunk people hunted and trapped muskrats for **pelts**.

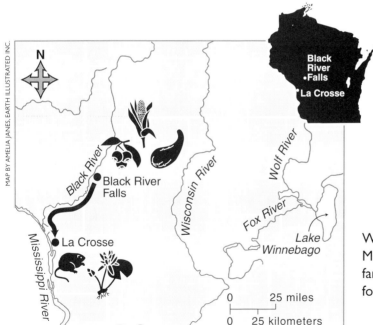

Why was it important that Mountain Wolf Woman's family collect most of their food in spring and summer?

slough: a swampy area near a river   **pelt:** an animal's skin with the hair or fur still on it

Muskrat

Muskrats also provided a dark red and nutritious meat. Mountain Wolf Woman's mother and aunts roasted them on a rack over a large fire. Many years later, as an old woman, Mountain Wolf Woman still remembered the sights and sounds and smells of those spring days. "The muskrat meat made a lot of noise," she said, as it sizzled and cooked. She remembered watching brown grease drip into the flames as Bends the Bough turned the muskrats over with a long, pointed stick. After the muskrats were cooked and cooled, the women packed and stored them to eat later during the summer.

Sometimes Mountain Wolf Woman's father fished in the spring. One spring, when she was only about 2 years old, her family was camping near Black River Falls. Her father caught a gigantic fish, a sturgeon. There are different ways to catch fish; some people use nets, and some use hooks. To get this

Fishermen spearing sturgeon

fish, her father used a spear. The fish was so big that its tail dragged on the ground as he carried it over his shoulder! Today, there are few sturgeon left in the Mississippi and Wisconsin rivers. The Department of Natural Resources protects them.

During the spring, Mountain Wolf Woman and her mother and sisters also dug for the roots of yellow water lilies. This was another good food. They went to sloughs covered with the shiny, dark green leaves of water lilies. Once there, they put on old dresses, took off their shoes, and waded into the cool water. They used their feet to find the large, fleshy roots—letting the river mud ooze through their toes until they found the roots they wanted. Then they used their feet to pull the roots free from the bottom, and the roots floated to the surface. Mountain Wolf Woman and her mother and sisters put the roots into large sacks and carried them back to camp.

Water lilies

At camp, sitting outside their wigwams, they scraped off the outside layer and then sliced the roots. Mountain Wolf Woman said they looked much like bananas. They strung the slices on string and hung them to dry. Then they stored the dried roots in large sacks. Later in the summer, the women cooked these dried roots with meat. Many years later, Mountain Wolf Woman recalled, "They were really delicious."

In the late spring, Mountain Wolf Woman's family returned to the log house on their homestead. Her mother and father planted and cared for a large garden. They also picked the wild blueberries growing in the woods around their home.

Lots of blueberries grew in the shade under the tall pine trees. Mountain Wolf Woman remembered that all of the Ho-Chunk picked blueberries back then. Mountain Wolf Woman and her mother dried some of the blueberries. During the winter, they boiled these dried berries with dried corn.

Loading blueberries (in boxes) in Black River Falls

Mountain Wolf Woman's family also picked blueberries to sell in town to earn money. Sometimes her father gave gum to the children, so they would chew gum and not eat the berries as they picked them. What a smart dad! Her family put the berries into square wooden boxes and took them into town to sell. The boxes had rope straps so her family members could carry the boxes on their backs or sling them over the backs of horses.

Mountain Wolf Woman thought they got a good price for blueberries—50 cents a quart at the beginning of the season! Back then, you could buy a lot more with 50 cents than you can today. Selling food that they gathered, such as blueberries, was a way that Ho-Chunk families earned money to buy other foods, household goods, and sometimes even horses. After they sold their blueberries,

Mountain Wolf Woman could have bought 5 *pounds* of candy with 50 cents! How much candy can you get with 50 cents?

Downtown Black River Falls where Mountain Wolf Woman and her family would have shopped with the money made from picking blueberries

Mountain Wolf Woman and her family put the store-bought items in the wooden boxes that had held the blueberries and headed back home.

When the corn was ripe, Mountain Wolf Woman and her family harvested it from their garden and carried it back to their house on their backs. They did not have big machines to pick the corn or trucks to haul it. To cook the corn, they dug a large pit in the ground, put in stones, and then made a big fire in the pit to heat the stones. When the stones were very, very hot, they took out the wood and smoldering ashes and put in corn husks. Next they added the ripe corn and covered it with more husks. Then Mountain Wolf Woman and her family covered the whole pit with dirt except for some holes to add water. When the water hit the rocks, "We used to hear the red hot stones make a rumbling sound," she remembered.

Harvesting corn

The next morning, Mountain Wolf Woman and her family carefully opened the pit and took out the hot cooked corn. Sometimes friends would come to help spread out the hot corn on a cloth placed on the ground. Some friends used clamshells to scrape the corn kernels off the cobs. Other friends used metal teaspoons. After the corn kernels dried in the sun, they were put into sacks. But Mountain Wolf Woman's family always left some corn on the stalks back in the fields. They saved this corn to use for seeds in the next spring's planting. It meant food for the future.

Corn ready for the fire pit

On other summer days, Mountain Wolf Woman helped her mother and sisters harvest squash from their garden. They wanted to save this food

Corn stalk

to use during the winter, so it had to be dried to keep it from rotting. First, they needed a drying rack. But they didn't go out to a garage or down in a basement to get a rack. Nor did they go to the store to buy one. They made a rack themselves.

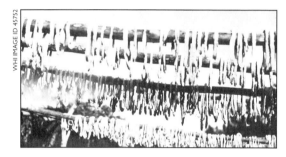

Squash drying on racks

Mountain Wolf Woman and her sisters went into the woods and found small trees that had forked branches. They took these branches, stuck them in the ground where they wanted their rack, and hung another branch between them. Then they peeled the squash, cut the squash into rings, strung the squash on the racks, and let the sun and air do their drying work.

During the summer, Mountain Wolf Woman, her grandmother, and her aunt also gathered Indian potatoes, sometimes known as groundnuts. These were not part of their garden. The Indian potatoes grew wild. But Mountain Wolf Woman and her family knew where to look for the potatoes because they knew the land and the plants so well. They found the potatoes in the woods, hidden among hazel bushes, in wet areas near creeks.

The Indian potatoes grew on long vines all strung together like a charm bracelet. These vines ran in all directions. When they found a vine, they dug out a whole string of potatoes. They cut the potatoes off the vines and then dried them. When the family needed these potatoes for food, Mountain Wolf Woman and her mother boiled them in water with some sugar until the water was all gone. Then they peeled off the skins and ate.

Mountain Wolf Woman's aunt and grandmother once told her about another way they used to gather food in Nebraska—stealing from mice! Mice stored foods like wild beans. But their supplies weren't safe from the Ho-Chunk women! They followed the tiny trails that mice left to storage holes in the ground. They said that sometimes they found a bucketful of beans, but Mountain Wolf Woman always wondered how big a bucket they meant.

The vines that Mountain Wolf Woman and her family looked for when hunting Indian potatoes

In thinking back on her summer days as a child, Mountain Wolf Woman said simply, "When various foods were ripe, the people dried them." In the summer, the Ho-Chunk grew and picked and dried many foods. During the warm months, Mountain Wolf Woman and her family were always working because they had to be thinking ahead. They had to make sure they would also have enough food in the winter and early spring, the time of year when it was most difficult to find food.

Mountain Wolf Woman and her family did not live in a house or apartment with an electric refrigerator like we have now. They did not even have an icebox like some families had back then. They did not have lots of cupboards and shelves with boxes and bags of **nonperishable** (non **pair** ish ubl) **foods.** Mountain Wolf Woman and her family dried their own foods and dug holes in the ground to bury foods that they planned to eat later. Storing the food below ground kept it safe from insects and other animals. When they needed food, Mountain Wolf Woman remembered that the adults would say, "Dig up that which is buried."

nonperishable food: food not easily spoiled

4

Following the Seasons: Fall and Winter

In the fall, after the work in the gardens was over, Mountain Wolf Woman and her family usually went to pick cranberries. This was another way to make money. When they arrived at a cranberry marsh, there often would be many Ho-Chunk families camping together. And everybody would pick berries—women, men, and children. The adults carried bushel-sized boxes at their sides. As they worked their way across the marsh, they left behind rows of filled boxes. Mountain Wolf Woman and the other children used small pails and picked the berries by hand and then put their

Cranberries

Ho-Chunk group harvesting cranberries

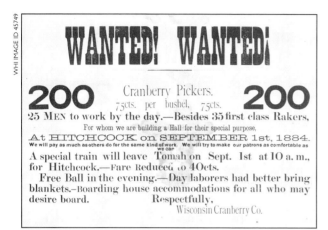

Notice for cranberry pickers

berries into their mothers' boxes. At noon, some would go back to camp to eat, but others brought lunches along and ate out in the marsh. Mountain Wolf Woman thought it was a lot of fun to pack a lunch and eat outside.

Mountain Wolf Woman really loved it when **peddlers** came to the cranberry marsh to sell things. Her favorites were the pies. She thought pies were great because her own family used to cook on campfires and could not bake pies and cakes. These baked goods were a real treat!

After cranberry-picking time, it was time for the fall move to hunt deer. Hunting deer is what Mountain Wolf Woman's family and other Ho-Chunk families always did in the fall, just as their ancestors had done before them for countless years.

peddler: a traveling salesperson

One place that they liked to hunt was in the woods outside of Neillsville, northeast of Black River Falls. There, Mountain Wolf Woman's family and 4 or 5 other families would build wigwams. Her grandmother and mother made their wigwam and covered it with mats of woven cattails. The other families were her sisters and their husbands and children as well as other relatives. Mountain Wolf Woman loved being with her family. Mountain Wolf Woman's family had so many people that they lived in a wigwam with 2 fireplaces. On cold nights, her father kept the fires going all night long, but the inside of the well-made wigwam was never too smoky. It was a good place to live.

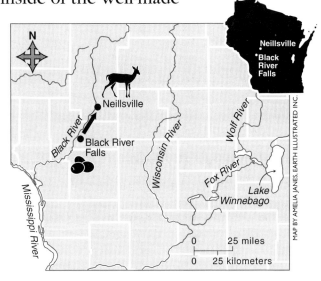

In the fall, Mountain Wolf Woman's family left home to hunt deer.

Mats

Mats were important in Ho-Chunk culture. All the women owned mats that they had made themselves from cattail leaves or bulrush reeds. And all the young girls had to learn how to make mats. These woven mats had many uses. They were used as doors, to sit on, and to cover wigwams. They also spread mats on the ground to dry corn.

To make a mat out of bulrush reeds, the reeds had to be picked, cut, dried, cooked in boiling water, dried again, bundled up, dyed, and then woven. Some were decorated with geometric designs. It took a lot of time.

Wood strips were woven together to make mats.

Close-up of finished mat

Needles used to make mats

Hunting was considered men's work, so only the men and boys hunted. When still young, boys learned how to hunt many kinds of animals from squirrels and rabbits to deer and bear. Mountain Wolf Woman remembered that the hunters used to find deer quickly. They always brought home some meat the first day. Back then, there were not as many hunters. Nobody needed a deer license. Her family killed as many deer as it needed. And sometimes it needed a lot! When Mountain Wolf Woman's father and other hunters shot a deer, they wrapped it in leaves and carried the deer back to camp on their backs. Occasionally, they even brought back a bear.

After hunting for a while in one place, sometimes the family would move its camp to hunt somewhere else. Mountain Wolf Woman's father, mother, and older sisters and brothers all carried packs on their backs to make the move. One year, though, they got a pony, and the pony carried all of their belongings when they moved their camp. Sometimes the children got to ride on top of the pack. Do you think a pony could carry all of your family's belongings? How many ponies do you think it would take?

Mountain Wolf Woman and her sisters and brothers used to fast during the time when the family was hunting. Among the Ho-Chunk people, fasting was a way to ask the spirits for a good life and sometimes to get power. Her parents encouraged all of their children to fast. Her brother Big Winnebago fasted from the fall to the early spring. During these months, he would not eat anything during the day. He would eat only after the sun went down.

Mountain Wolf Woman and her older sister Distant Flashes Standing fasted, too. When their father left in the morning to hunt, Mountain Wolf Woman and Distant Flashes Standing took coals from old, cold fires and blackened their cheeks. Blackening their faces was part of the fasting **ritual.** They fasted to receive blessings, and they blackened their cheeks so people would know not to offer them food.

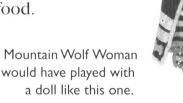

Mountain Wolf Woman would have played with a doll like this one.

ritual: an action that is always done the same way as part of a ceremony or tradition

Distant Flashes Standing sat indoors and wove yarn belts, but Mountain Wolf Woman liked to play outside. At the end of the day, when their father returned from hunting, he used to say to them, "Go cry to the Thunders," which meant, go pray to the spirits. And when he was ready to eat, he gave the girls tobacco and again told them to go pray. To the Ho-Chunk people and members of other Indian nations, tobacco is a **sacred** (**sa** cred) plant. Tobacco has special significance and is used as an offering to the spirits.

Tobacco plant

Mountain Wolf Woman and her sister went into the woods and looked at the dark night sky and cried to the Thunders. They sang, "Oh, good spirits. Will they pity me? Here I am, pleading." They sang this because if the spirits had pity—that is, if the spirits felt sorry for them—then the spirits would give them a blessing. The girls then scattered tobacco and looked at the moon and stars. Thinking back on those times, Mountain Wolf Woman said, "We used to cry because, after all, we were hungry. We used to think we were pitied. We really wanted to mean what we were saying." Then they went home and ate.

sacred: something deserving of respect

At night in the wigwam, Mountain Wolf Woman's father told the children to prepare their bedding and lie down. There were no television sets or even radios, but her father told wonderful stories. These were good memories for Mountain Wolf Woman. She said, "I really enjoyed listening to my father tell stories." Everyone in the whole family stayed quiet so that they could hear all of the words. The stories he told were sacred to the Ho-Chunk people. Many years later, Mountain Wolf Woman still thought fondly of these stories even though she said, "I do not know all of them any more, I just remember parts."

She remembered one story about a Ho-Chunk man getting **revenge** after another tribe had killed everyone in his town. This man snuck into the other tribe's town during the night and cut off the heads of the chief's son and daughter-in-law! And then he took their heads and went up to the moon. Mountain Wolf Woman's father told her that on nights when the moon was full, she could look up and see the man carrying the 2 heads in his hand. Go check out the next full moon. What do you see?

revenge: getting even

Hunting came to an end when the winter was at its coldest and there was a lot of snow. It was then that Mountain Wolf Woman and her family left their hunting camp and went back to their home near Black River Falls. They spent the coldest winter months warm in their own log house.

After the hunting season, it was time for the winter feast. Seasonal feasts and ceremonies played a big part in Mountain Wolf Woman's childhood. Feasts were important ways that Ho-Chunk people made offerings to the spirits. Spring, fall, and winter feasts were also known as war-bundle feasts or ceremonies.

Lacrosse was a game enjoyed by many Wisconsin Indians. Ho-Chunk men and women played it on ceremonial occasions.

War Bundles

Many generations in the past, ancestors tied the first war bundles. War bundles consist of animal skins or hides wrapped around items important to a family. The bundles contain items such as pipes, feathers, animal bones, and, in more recent times, such things as soldiers' medals. Succeeding generations add to the bundle. The war bundle offers protection and blessings to the entire family group.

The items in the center are part of the war bundle.

Mountain Wolf Woman remembered that her father used to give large feasts. He built a special long wigwam for the winter feast. And for this work, her father had help from his nephews. Remember, for the Ho-Chunk, relationships among family members mean particular duties and privileges. Nephews are expected to work for their uncles, that is, their mother's brothers. (Among the Ho-Chunk, father's brothers were called father, not uncle.)

Mountain Wolf Woman remembered one winter feast that was held in a wigwam long enough to hold 8 fireplaces! Many Ho-Chunk people came, so Mountain Wolf Woman's father fed a whole wigwam full of people. Mountain Wolf Woman remembered that he provided 10 deer for one such feast! Many deer meant people could make offerings to more spirits. The winter feast lasted overnight. People gave speeches, danced, and sang, and they offered tobacco, specially prepared deer hides, and prayers to the spirits. It was a time for clan members to come together. Mountain Wolf Woman enjoyed being part of this large family group.

Ho-Chunk dressed in their ceremonial clothes

Sometimes people fasted before feasts and then broke their fasts at the feast. Mountain Wolf Woman remembered a time when her brothers Big Winnebago and Strikes Standing fasted in the woods before a feast. Boys fasted to **obtain a vision**. Mountain Wolf Woman's father built a shelter for them to live in, and they were supposed to stay there all by themselves for 4 nights! But Strikes Standing did not have the patience to wait 4 nights, and he came home early. Bends the Bough was upset with him for not following this tradition,

obtain a vision: find a spirit to help throughout life

and she cried. Like all parents, perhaps even your own, she was worried that her child was making wrong choices. But Big Winnebago stayed until it was feast time.

Despite all of their hunting, gathering, and gardening during the year, sometimes Mountain Wolf Woman's family did not have much food. In remembering his own childhood, Big Winnebago said that was why he became such a fast eater. The family always ate out of just one dish, so he learned to eat quickly to get enough. How would your family do if you had to hunt, plant, and gather all of your food? You might have hungry times, too.

5
Many Ways of Growing Up

Throughout Mountain Wolf Woman's childhood, her family usually followed the same cycle—spring, summer, fall, and winter. But when it was almost fall of the year that Mountain Wolf Woman was 9, her oldest brother said that she should go to school! He said that he liked to hear women speak English. He thought his little sister should learn how to speak it. Among the Ho-Chunk, big brothers made decisions for their sisters. Can you imagine how your life would be if your older brother made decisions for you?

It was then that Mountain Wolf Woman's parents let her go to school in Tomah. It was a special government school just for Indian people. It tried to teach them to be more like non-Indian people. Mountain Wolf Woman went to this school for 2 years, but then she didn't go again for a long time. Mountain Wolf Woman said her family did not stay home just so the children could attend school. Back then, hunting and gathering and helping your family were more important. Her family's travels took her away from Tomah and school.

Main building of the Tomah Indian Industrial School

Mountain Wolf Woman and her family continued their yearly cycle. In the fall and winter, they went hunting and picked cranberries, and in the springtime, they returned to the Mississippi River to catch muskrats and dig lilies. One year, though, when they returned to their home near Black River Falls, her mother and father said that they were not going to plant their summer garden. Instead, the family was going to Wittenberg to help her father's uncles. They were old and could no longer help themselves. As you know, among the Ho-Chunk, nephews were expected to help their uncles.

To move to Wittenberg, the family didn't call a moving company, get into a car, and ride down a highway. They moved themselves. They used big wagons pulled by horses. This was a long journey by horse—almost 100 miles! On the way to Wittenberg, they stopped at a Ho-Chunk and Potawatomi (pah tah **wah** tuh me) Indian settlement in the woods north of Marshfield. Mountain Wolf Woman's mother and father both had relatives there. It was a good place for Indians to live the way they wanted. They could follow their own traditions and not worry about non-Indians interfering. Mountain Wolf Woman and her family stayed 2 nights in order to visit with family and rest the horses.

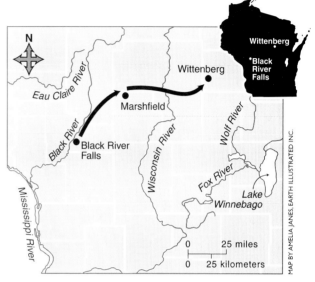

Mountain Wolf Woman's family made this trip by horse and wagon.

Mountain Wolf Woman stayed in a house with an aunt and her husband. Aunts were expected to treat their nieces and nephews with great generosity, and indeed they did! The sisters of Mountain Wolf Woman's father gave them gifts of maple sugar in a handwoven bag. The maple sugar was in cakes of hardened syrup. The aunts also gave them a sack of powdered maple sugar. These were wonderful gifts! In return, Mountain Wolf Woman's mother gave her sisters-in-law necklaces, bracelets, and long earrings that had coins dangling on the ends.

Ho-Chunk necklace and bracelet

Once they arrived at Wittenberg, Mountain Wolf Woman and her family stopped at the log cabin of one of her grandfathers, High Snake. He was a member of the Snake Clan. Then her father went and got his 2 elderly uncles, Good Snake and Fear the Snake Den, and brought them to High Snake's place. (Good Snake and Fear the Snake Den were also Mountain Wolf

Woman's grandfathers. Among the Ho-Chunk, grandfathers were not just your mother's and father's father but also included other relatives like the brothers of grandparents.)

Mountain Wolf Woman's father and his uncles were members of a **medicine lodge**. Mountain Wolf Woman's father helped Good Snake and Fear the Snake Den cut trees for poles. Then they built a wigwam used for medicine lodge ceremonies. The size of the wigwam varied for these ceremonies; it depended on how many people were expected to attend. When her father and his uncles finished the east end of the wigwam—the side where the sun rose—they sang.

Membership in a medicine lodge was not decided by who you were related to. You had to be invited to join. Members of the medicine lodge taught the people who joined about how the earth and all the animals were formed by the Earthmaker. They also told about how people were unhappy until they learned the proper way to live—the medicine lodge way. Members believed that following the ways of the medicine lodge helped them have good health and a long life.

medicine lodge: an organization of people who practice special ceremonies together

Many Ho-Chunk people came to the medicine lodge that Mountain Wolf Woman's father and his uncles had built. Some walked. Some came on horseback. And some arrived in horse-drawn wagons. On this occasion, Mountain Wolf Woman's older sister White Thunder and her older brother Strikes Standing were **initiated** (ih **nih** she ay ted) into the medicine lodge with a special ceremony.

What Is Traditional Ho-Chunk Medicine?

Among the Ho-Chunk, traditional "medicine" did not mean pills or shots or doctor's visits. Medicines were sacred or holy. They could be parts of plants or animals and used for many purposes besides just curing illnesses. For example, there were medicines to provide success in hunts, to make one rich, and to find a husband or wife.

Cutting roots for medicine

A raspberry bark bunch used for medicine

initiated: made someone a member of a group or club

After the medicine lodge, someone said that people in town were paying money for the bark of slippery elm trees. Slippery elm bark was used to treat a variety of conditions, from wounds to intestinal problems. Mountain Wolf Woman's father decided they needed to earn some money, so they collected and sold slippery elm bark, too. Those in the family who were strong and could work packed a wagon with some household goods. Then they went looking for slippery elm in the woods. Mothers and younger children, including Mountain Wolf Woman, set up camp near their grandfather's house and waited for the others to return.

Slippery elm tree

When her father and the others found slippery elm, they asked the owners of the land where they found it if they could take the bark. The owners agreed that they could. Mountain Wolf Woman's father and the others peeled the gummy bark off the trees. They cut the bark in strips as long as their arms and then tied the strips into bundles. When everyone had a bundle, they put them on their backs and returned to where they were camping in the woods.

The women peeled off the outer bark with knives and hung the inner bark on drying racks. They dried a lot of bark and tied it into bundles. And then they took the bundles into towns and sold the slippery elm to **pharmacists**. Those who worked getting the slippery elm then got a chance to visit the rest of their families. They brought their families food before going back to the forest to gather more bark. But this way of making money did not last long for Mountain Wolf Woman's family. After a while, the landowners who owned the trees wanted to keep everything for themselves and no longer let the Ho-Chunk people gather the bark.

And then it was fall. Some of Mountain Wolf Woman's sisters returned to Black River Falls, but her father, mother, brothers, and older sister Distant Flashes Standing did not go back. One of her grandfathers, named Rattlesnake, said that they should live in Wittenberg near him. There, her father built a big, round wigwam where they stayed for a while.

pharmacist: someone who prepares and sells drugs and medicines

Later that fall, her father decided it was time to go trapping, so the entire family, including the grandfathers, moved to Green Lake to trap. When it started to get really cold, they went back to Wittenberg. Only then did Mountain Wolf Woman finally get to go back to school. She was 13. She went to the Lutheran Mission School at Wittenberg. There she was baptized as a Christian. But she also held on to some Ho-Chunk beliefs. Mountain Wolf Woman used to say, "Whatever is good, that I would do."

Around this time, Mountain Wolf Woman's older brothers found another way to make money—dancing in shows! People in towns would pay to see traditional Indian dances. And so her

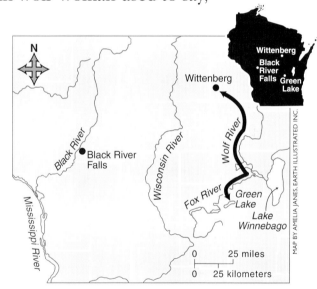

Do you think Mountain Wolf Woman felt a long way from home in Wittenberg and Green Lake, or do you think she felt all of Wisconsin was home as long as she was with her family?

Lutheran Mission School at Wittenberg

brothers traveled to places like Milwaukee; Chicago, Illinois; and St. Paul, Minnesota, to dance in shows.

Big Winnebago used some of the money he made to buy Mountain Wolf Woman a bicycle. This brotherly gift followed an old tradition. Long ago, Ho-Chunk brothers brought home items won in battles for their sisters. Many years later, Mountain Wolf Woman remembered being so proud of that bike. No other student in her school had one. She was the first!

At the Lutheran Mission School, Mountain Wolf Woman became friends with Nancy, an Oneida Indian woman who taught sewing. Nancy had a bicycle, too. When there were social dances (dances just for fun), sometimes the 2 of them would ride their bikes together to the dance. One time, though, they went the old-fashioned way—they hired 2 horses and rode! The horses were hard to handle, and so they let them run and run until they were tired.

When they got to the dance, Mountain Wolf Woman just sat and watched. All of the dancers were dressed in their jewelry and best traditional Ho-Chunk clothes. Then a friend asked her to dance, and dance she did! She really loved to dance and wasn't embarrassed that she was wearing what she called "citizen's clothing." This meant she was dressed like a non-Indian girl, but she didn't care. She loved to dance.

One day, Mountain Wolf Woman's family took her out of school and told her that it was time for her to be married. Although she was an older teenager, she hadn't even finished sixth grade! She cried because she liked school, and she

Women and girls in traditional Ho-Chunk jewelry and clothes

didn't want to get married. But back then, Mountain Wolf Woman had to do what her family said. Her older brother had arranged a marriage with a man he knew. Mountain Wolf Woman could not disobey. She expected her brothers to arrange her marriage because that was the custom among the Ho-Chunk. Still, she was upset because her brother had not made a good match. He had not talked about it with her at all. She grew angry. But her mother said, "Daughter, I prize you

Mountain Wolf Woman: A Ho-Chunk Girlhood

Mountain Wolf Woman around the time she got married

very much, but this matter cannot be helped. When you are older and know better, you can marry whomever you yourself think that you want to marry." Mountain Wolf Woman did not forget that. She also promised herself that her own children could choose whom to marry, and they did!

For Mountain Wolf Woman's arranged marriage, Bends the Bough combed her daughter's hair and dressed her in a skirt and shawl with ribbon embroidery. Her mother also gave her a necklace, earrings, and a pony to ride. And that was how she looked when she first met her new husband, the son of a man called Pine. Mountain Wolf Woman and her husband rode together on the pony to where his family lived. All of his female relatives were there waiting for them. What a mix of emotions she must have felt—a bit scared, probably, and maybe still a bit angry.

But Mountain Wolf Woman knew what she was supposed to do because her mother had taught her well. She went into a wigwam, laid down her shawl, took off the clothes and the jewelry that she was wearing, and put them on the shawl. Then her new mother-in-law came into the wigwam, took the shawl, and gave away the clothes and jewelry to the relatives waiting outside. But each relative who got something gave something in return to Mountain Wolf Woman. After 2 or 3 days, Mountain Wolf Woman rode back to her own family with 4 horses and a shawl so full of things that she could barely tie the corners shut! Later, 2 more horses were delivered. That was how Ho-Chunk marriages were done back in the old days. There was not a religious ceremony. Families exchanged gifts instead.

Afterword

When she was grown up, Mountain Wolf Woman left her first husband and married a man that her oldest brother, Crashing Thunder, recommended. In all, she had 11 children and lived in Wisconsin, Nebraska, South Dakota, and Oregon. She had a busy life. Mountain Wolf Woman continued to do many of the things she had done as a child—plant vegetable gardens, pick blueberries and cranberries, make mats, sew and cook, and go to feasts and dance. She also learned Indian medicines from a grandfather and worked as a **midwife**, helping other women have their babies.

Mountain Wolf Woman's children had children, and these children have had children! Today, Mountain Wolf Woman's **descendants** include nurses, schoolteachers, and bookkeepers. Some work for the Ho-Chunk Nation making sure that the Ho-Chunk people and their traditions continue to thrive in their homeland, the land we call Wisconsin.

midwife: someone who helps women when they have their babies   **descendants:** someone's children and grandchildren and their children and grandchildren

Afterword

Mountain Wolf Woman lived to be 76 years old. Through these years, she saw many changes around her. She herself also changed. In 1958, Mountain Wolf Woman flew to Ann Arbor, Michigan, and spent 5 weeks with her adopted niece, anthropologist Nancy Lurie. Mountain Wolf Woman liked the running water at Nancy Lurie's house. But she did not trust the electric stove because she was used to cooking over an open fire outdoors or with a wood-burning oven.

Sometimes, when Lurie was out of the house, Mountain Wolf Woman made her own meals in the living room fireplace and baked bread in the hot coals. At the age of 73, she even chopped the firewood! During those weeks, Mountain Wolf Woman shared her life stories with her niece. Because she did, people today know who Mountain Wolf Woman was and how she lived.

Mountain Wolf Woman in her later years

Appendix

Mountain Wolf Woman's Time Line

1874 — In the winter, Mountain Wolf Woman's family is moved to Nebraska by the U.S. government, where they stay until spring. They return to Wisconsin by traveling down the Missouri River and then back up the Mississippi River.

1884 — Mountain Wolf Woman is born in April.

1893–1895 — At 9 years old, Mountain Wolf Woman goes to school for the first time at the Tomah Indian Industrial School. She goes to the school for only 2 years.

1897–1898 — Mountain Wolf Woman is 13 when she returns to school and attends the Lutheran Mission School in Wittenberg.

1958 — Mountain Wolf Woman visits her adopted niece, anthropologist Nancy Lurie, in Ann Arbor, Michigan. She tells Nancy Lurie about what her life was like as a Ho-Chunk girl.

1960 — Mountain Wolf Woman dies at age 76.

Glossary

algae (**al** jee): small plants with roots or stems that live in water or on damp surfaces

ancestor: a family member from long ago

anthropologist (an thro **pah** lo jist): a scientist who studies human history by looking at the languages people speak; the environment in which they live; and the way they work, dress, eat, create art, and construct buildings

archaeologist (ar key **ol** o jist): a scientist who learns about the past by studying artifacts or objects left behind at places where people once lived, worked, and played

ceremonial (ser uh **mo** nee uhl): formal or traditional

ceremony (**ser** uh mo nee): the formal words, actions, or songs that mark an important special occasion, such as a wedding or a funeral

clan: a group of people with a common sacred ancestor, such as an animal or spirit

cradleboard: a baby carrier used by American Indians

cultivating: growing crops

culture: the way of life, ideas, and traditions of a group of people

descendants: someone's children and grandchildren and their children and grandchildren

dugout canoe: a boat made by hollowing out a large log

fast: go without food

generosity: helping others by sharing things such as time or money

granulate: form crystals

homestead: land given by the U.S. government to settlers if they built a home and began farming within 5 years

initiated (ih **nih** she ay ted): made someone a member of a group or club

medicine lodge: an organization of people who practice special ceremonies together

midwife: someone who helps women when they have their babies

nonperishable (non **pair** ish ubl) **food**: food not easily spoiled

obtain a vision: find a spirit to help throughout life

origin: where something comes from

peddler: a traveling salesperson

pelt: an animal's skin with the hair or fur still on it

Glossary

pharmacist: someone who prepares and sells drugs and medicines

privilege: a special right

reservation: federal land reserved or set aside for Indian nations to live on

revenge: getting even

ritual: an action that is always done the same way as part of a ceremony or tradition

sacred (**sa** cred): something deserving of respect

slough (sloo): a swampy area near a river

spiritual (**spir** i choo el): something that has to do with the soul and the spirit

tasseling: when the tassel, the part of a corn stalk with pollen on it, appears

translated: put in a different language

treaty: an official, written agreement between nations

tuber: a root or bulb

wigwam: a home made of cattail mats or tree bark attached to a framework of small branches

Reading Group Guide and Activities

Discussion Questions

- Mountain Wolf Woman had a very early memory when she was still young enough to be carried in a cradleboard. What is your earliest memory? What do your friends say are their earliest memories? Why do you think these events stand out in your memory and the memories of your friends?

- Family was very important to Mountain Wolf Woman. Among the Ho-Chunk, family relationships had both duties and privileges. Think back over Mountain Wolf Woman's life. How did she help family members? How did they help her? Think about your own family. How do your relationships with family members differ from Mountain Wolf Woman's relationships with her family members?

- For each season of the year, Mountain Wolf Woman and her family participated in different activities like digging for yellow water lilies in the spring and picking cranberries in the fall. What are some of the things that you and your family and friends do in different seasons? Why do you think you do some things in summer and others in winter? Describe your favorite seasonal activity.

Activities and Projects

- Imagine that there are no grocery stores and you have to live off what you can hunt or gather or plant! What would you eat? Where would you find it? Use the library and the Internet to research where your favorite foods are grown and/or produced. Then take a map of the U.S. and decide where you would need to go to get what you want.

- Reread the section in Chapter 2 on Ho-Chunk names and how Mountain Wolf Woman got her ceremonial name. Ask your parents how you got your name. Pick a place—your city or town or a nearby river or lake—and find out how the place got its name. Ask your local historical society for help.

- Mountain Wolf Woman and her family did many of the same things that the Ho-Chunk people had done for generations. Interview someone in your family, like an aunt or grandfather, about family traditions that they followed as children then passed on to *their* children.

- Go to a Ho-Chunk Pow Wow and watch the dancing! Or view the *New Dawn of Tradition* video at http://ecb.org/wisconsin/powwow. Describe how this dancing is different from other dancing you have seen. How is it similar?

To Learn More about the Ho-Chunk

Hieb, Jane A., ed. *Visions and Voices: Winnebago Elders Speak to the Children*. Independence, WI: Western Dairyland Economic Opportunity Council, 1994.

Hunter, Sally A. *Four Seasons of Corn: A Winnebago Tradition*. Minneapolis, MN: Lerner Publications, 1997.

Kallen, Stuart A. *Native Americans of the Great Lakes*. San Diego, CA: Lucent Books, 2000.

Loew, Patty. "The Ho-Chunk Nation." Chapter 4 in *Native People of Wisconsin*. Madison, WI: Wisconsin Historical Society Press, 2003.

Milwaukee Public Museum. "Indian Country Wisconsin." http://www.mpm.edu/wirp.

Mountain Wolf Woman. *Mountain Wolf Woman: Sister of Crashing Thunder; The Autobiography of a Winnebago Indian*. Edited by Nancy Oestreich Lurie. Ann Arbor: University of Michigan Press, 1961.

Thunder in the Dells. VHS. Directed by Dave Erickson. Lone Rock, WI: Ootek Productions, 1991.

Acknowledgments

I thank Bobbie Malone, Director of the Office of School Services, for inviting me to undertake this project. Her enthusiasm for history and gift of sharing this enthusiasm with young people make working with her a joy. I also thank the WHS editorial staff, Elizabeth Boone and Erica Schock, for asking good questions and providing consistency. John Zimm did excellent photo research for the project, aided by WHS colleague John Nondorf and Jennifer Kolb and Diana Zlatanovski at the Wisconsin Historical Museum. State Archaeologist John Broihahn helpfully dealt with every question tossed his way. Jill Bremigan added to the story's intrigue through her outstanding design of the book, and Diane Drexler deftly guided the book through production.

Most of all, I thank Dr. Nancy Oestreich Lurie, who graciously read the manuscript and offered many clarifying insights to help bring Mountain Wolf Woman's story to a new generation of readers. I also thank Frances Thundercloud Wentz, who originally translated Mountain Wolf Woman's words for Dr. Lurie, for helping us with the translation of the Ho-Chunk terms in this book. Many many thanks to all involved.

Index

Page numbers in **bold** means that there is a picture on that page.

A

ancestors, 1, 15
animal spirits, 15

B

baby carriers. *See* cradleboards
Bald Eagle (sister), 20
baskets, **23**
beadwork, **4**, **54**
Bear Clan, 15
bears, 42, **42**
Bends the Bough (mother)
   on following tradition, 49-50
   homestead of, 14
   before Mountain Wolf Woman's birth, 7-8, 14
   Mountain Wolf Woman's childhood and, 17, 18, 21
   on Mountain Wolf Woman's marriage, 63
   resettlement of, 7-8
   return to Wisconsin of, 9, 11-13
berry picking
   blueberries, 26, 30-33, **31**
   cranberries, **38**, 38-39, **39**

Big Winnebago (brother), 20, 43, 49-50
Black River Falls, Wisconsin, 11, 14, **14**, 27, **31**, **32**
British settlers, 5

C

canoes. *See* dugout canoes
ceremonies, 46
   See also feasts
cattail. *See* mats
clans, 13, 15, **15**
   See also specific clans
clothes, traditional, **23**, **49**, 61, **62**, 63, 64
corn, **33**, 33-34, **34**
cradleboards, 18, 19, **19**
Crashing Thunder (brother), 20

D

dancing, 48, 60, 61
deer, 39-40, 42, 48
Department of Natural Resources, 29
Distant Flashes Standing (sister), 20, 43-44, 58
dolls, **43**
dugout canoes, 9-11, **10**

E

Eagle Clan, 14, 15
earth clan, 15
Earthmaker, 23, 55
education
    at home, 22-23
    at school, 51-52, **59**, 59-61, **60**
European settlers, 3, 5
    trade with, 4-5, 10

F

fall activities
    cranberry picking, **38**, 38-39, **39**
    hunting, 26, 39-40, **40**, 42-43
family roles
    aunts, 2, 54
    brothers, 51, 60, 62-63
    duties and privileges, 2, 48
    grandfathers, 54
    nephews, 2, 48, 53, 54
    nieces, 2, 53
    sisters, 51, 60
    uncles, 48, 53
fasting, 22, 43, 49-50
Fear the Snake Den (grandfather), 54-56
feasts, 46, 48-50
fishing, 28-29, **29**
food, 3, 26, **27**, 37, 50
    See also specific methods of obtaining
Fox River, 4, 6
French settlers, 3, 4, 12

G

gardening, 3, **4**, 26, 30
    corn, **33**, 33-34, **34**
    squash, 34-35, **35**
gathering, 3
    food stored by mice, 36
    potatoes, 35-36, 36
    slippery elm bark, 57, 57-58
    water lilies, 29-30, 30
generosity, as duty, 2, 21, 54, 60, 64
gifts, 21, 54, 60, 64
Good Snake (grandfather), 54-56
Green Bay, Wisconsin, 4, 6
Green Lake, 59, **59**
groundnuts. *See* potatoes

H

High Snake (grandfather), 54
Ho-Chunk
    language of, 6
    as name, 6
Ho-Chunk Nation
    history of in Wisconsin, 1, 4
    lands of, 7
    resettlement of by government, 5-7, 6, 13, 67
homesteads, 13-14
houses. *See* log cabin, wigwams
hunger, 50
hunting, 3, 26, 39-40, **40**, 42-43, 46

I

Iroquois, 3

J

jewelry, 54, **54**, **62**, 63

L

La Crosse, Wisconsin, 11, 27
lacrosse (game), **46**
land
   decisions about, 15
   Ho-Chunk territory, **7**
   as private property, 13, 26
log cabin, 14, 30
Lurie, Nancy Oestreich, 2, 18, 66, 67
Lutheran Mission School, 59-61, **60**, 67

M

maple sugar, 16-17, **17**, 54
marriage, 62-64, 65
Marshfield, Wisconsin, 53
marsh rabbits. *See* muskrats
mats, cattail, 3, 40, 41, **41**
   for wigwams, 9
medicine, traditional, **56**, 56-58, 65
medicine lodge, 55-56
Mississippi River, 11, 12, 27, 67
Missouri River, 9, 11, 12, 67
moccasins, **23**
month names, 25
Mountain Wolf Woman
   birth of, 1
   death of, 67
   descendants of, 65
   early childhood of, 16, 17-18, 21-22
   as a grown-up, 65-66, **66**
   life story collected, 2
   marriage of, 62-64, 65

   name of, 20-22
   religious beliefs of, 59
   school years of, 51-52, **59**, 59-61, **60**
   as a teenager, **viii**, **63**
Mountain Wolf Woman: Sister of Crashing Thunder; The Autobiography of a Winnebago Indian (Lurie), 2
muskrats, 27-28, **28**

N

names
   birth order and, 20
   ceremonial, 20, 21
   for Ho-Chunk Nation, 6
   of months, 25
Nebraska, Ho-Chunk people in, 5, 7, 9
Neillsville, Wisconsin, 40
Nicolet, Jean, 3, **3**

P

Pine (father-in-law), 64
potatoes, Indian, 35-36, **36**
Potawatomi, 53
Prairie du Chien, Wisconsin, 11
prayers and offerings, 44, 48

R

Rattlesnake (grandfather), 58-59
reservations, 5, 7
resettlement by government, 5-7, **6**, 13, 67
Revolutionary War, 5
River's Mouth Place, 11, 12

Index

S

seasonal cycles, 24–27, 52
　See also individual seasons
sky clan, 13, 14, 15
slippery elm, as medicine, **57**, 57–58
Snake Clan, 54
spear fishing, 29, **29**
spirits
　of clans, 15
　prayers and offerings to, 44, 48
　religion and, 23
spring activities, 13
　blueberry picking, 30–33
　fishing, 28–29, **29**
　maple sugar making, 16, 26
　trapping, 26, 27
　water lily gathering, 29–30
squash, 34–35, **35**
St. Louis, Missouri, 11, 12
store-bought items, 32–33
Strikes Standing (brother), 20, 49–50, 56
sturgeon, 28–29
sugaring. *See* maple sugar
summer activities
　gardening, 26, 30, **33**, 33–35, **34**, **35**
　gathering potatoes, 35–36, **36**

T

Thunder Clan, 13, 15
Thundercloud, Frances, 2
tobacco, 44, **44**, 48
Tomah Indian Industrial School, 51–52, **52**, 67
Tomah, Wisconsin, 51–52
tools, 10
trapping, 4, 27
treaties, 5

V

visions, obtaining, 49–50

W

war bundles, 46, 47, **47**
water lilies, 29–30, **30**
weaving, 44
White Thunder (sister), 17, 20, 56
wigwams, **8**, 8–9, 40, 48, 55
Winnebago
　as name, 6
　See also Ho-Chunk
winter activities
　feasts, 46, 48–50
　hunting, 26, 46
Wisconsin
　resettlement from, 5–7, **6**, 13, 67
　return to, 6, 9, 11–13, 67
　statehood of, 1
Wittenberg, Wisconsin, 52–53, **53**, 59, **59**
Wolf Clan, 21
Wolf Woman, 21–22